Tales of Edgar Allan Poe

Edgar Allan Poe

Abridged and adapted by Tony Napoli

Illustrated by Karen Loccisano

A PACEMAKER CLASSIC

GLOBE FEARON

Pearson Learning Group

Supervising Editor: Stephen Feinstein
Project Editor: Karen Bernhaut
Editorial Assistant: Stacie Dozier
Art Director: Nancy Sharkey
Assistant Art Director: Armando Baéz
Production Manager: Penny Gibson
Production Editor: Nicole Cypher
Desktop Specialist: Eric Dawson
Manufacturing Supervisor: Della Smith
Marketing Manager: Marge Curson
Cover Illustration: Karen Loccisano

ISBN 0-835-91069-5
Printed in the United States of America

  11 12 13   05 04

Globe
Fearon
Pearson Learning Group

1-800-321-3106
www.pearsonlearning.com

Contents

The Fall of the House of Usher

I had been riding alone on horseback during a dull, dark, and soundless day. It was autumn. As evening came, I found myself at last in sight of the House of Usher. I don't know why, but when I first saw the house I was filled with a terrible sense of gloom.

I looked at the house and the grounds. The house had bleak walls and empty eye-shaped windows. The grounds contained a few overgrown plants and the white trunks of dying trees. The whole scene made my heart sink.

I stood with my horse beside a dark and still lake at the base of the house. When I looked down at the water, I shuddered even more than before. The image of the same bleak house and dying tree trunks was thrown back at me.

I had come to this house to visit its owner, Roderick Usher. He had been one of my boyhood friends. But we hadn't seen each other in years. I had received a letter from him telling me that he was ill. He said he had a great need to see me, his best and only real friend. The feeling that went into his request left me no choice. I set out at once.

As boys we had spent much time together. But I never knew him well. He was not one to make close friendships. I did know a little about his family, however. They had been famous for many years for their works of art. And they were also known for their great deeds of charity. Their family history went back very far. So, after many generations, the name "House of Usher" was used to describe both the family and the family mansion.

I looked up at the house once more. As I did, a strange thought entered my mind. I began to believe that a dull, leaden-colored vapor hung about the entire mansion. It seemed to be separate from the natural air or atmosphere. It appeared to come up from the decayed trees and the gray walls and the silent lake.

I shook myself. I tried to put out of my mind what *must* have been a dream. I looked more closely at the mansion. It was quite old. Yet, while the individual stones were crumbling, no section of the building had fallen. But I did notice a slight crack in the walls. It began at the roof in front. And it ran in a zigzag direction down the wall until it became lost in the waters of the lake.

I rode over a short bridge to the mansion. A servant took my horse, and I entered a great hall. Another servant took me in silence through many dark and twisting passages to the master's study. On one of the staircases, I met the family doctor. He had a puzzled look on his face. He barely spoke to me and hurried on past. The servant threw open a door and led me in to his master.

The room I entered was very large, with a high ceiling. The windows were long, narrow, and pointed. And they were set so far above the floor that they were out of reach. Dark drapes hung on the walls. The furniture was old and worn and looked uncomfortable. Many books and musical instruments lay scattered about. But they failed to give life to the room. I felt I was breathing in air filled with sorrow and gloom.

When I came in, Usher got up from a sofa and greeted me warmly. At first I thought his friendliness was forced. When I looked at his face, however, I was sure he was sincere.

I gazed upon him with a mixed feeling of pity and awe. Never had a man changed so much in such a short period of time. I could not believe that this was the same person who had been my boyhood friend. Even then his looks had been strange. He had a pale face, with large, bright eyes. His lips were thin, and his nose was large. His hair had a weblike softness, and his forehead was very wide. Now these features stood out even more. And his skin was even paler.

His manner was odd, too. It was lively and nervous one moment, unsure the next. His voice changed often as well. It went from one of trembling doubt to one of hollow sureness.

He spoke of the purpose of my visit. He hoped I could provide him with the comfort he needed. Then he described at length the nature of his illness.

"It is a family evil," he said. "I cannot hope to find a cure." Then he added quickly, "It's just a nervous condition. It will soon pass off."

He then told me of the various symptoms of his sickness. The details interested and puzzled me.

"My senses are too sharp," he said. "I can eat only the most tasteless foods. I can wear only clothes made from a certain cloth. The smell of flowers is too strong for me. My eyes cannot stand even the softest light. And the only sounds that do not horrify me are those made by string instruments."

He waited for a moment and then went on. "Above all, I am a slave to an awful sense of FEAR," he said. "I will die, I *must* die in this folly. I shall have to give up life in some mighty struggle with FEAR."

I also learned something else of his mental condition. He had certain superstitions about the house in which he lived, and which he had not left in years. He felt the walls had some kind of a hold on his spirit and mind.

Finally he offered another, more understandable, reason for his state of mind. His beloved sister—his only companion for years—was seriously ill. The approaching death of his only living relative had much to do with his gloom.

"Her death," he said with a great bitterness, "will make me the last of the Ushers."

While he spoke, his sister—the Lady Madeline—passed slowly through a far section of the room. Then, without noticing me, she disappeared. My eyes followed her retreating steps. When a door closed behind her, I looked at her brother. He had buried his face in his hands and began to cry.

The nature of Lady Madeline's illness had long puzzled her doctors. She seemed to be simply wasting away. Up to now, she had fought her illness. But the night I arrived, she took to her bed. Usher told me that the glimpse I'd gotten of her would probably be the last time I would see her alive.

For several days, neither Usher nor I spoke of Lady Madeline. During that time I tried hard to relieve my friend's sadness. We painted and read together. Or I listened, as if in a dream, to the wild songs he played on his guitar. In so doing, I got closer and closer to him. As I did, I realized something. It was hopeless to try to cheer up a mind as dark as his.

The lengthy songs Usher played will ring forever in my ears. I remember discussing one particular song with him. It led us to a different topic. Usher held a belief that fascinated me. It wasn't because the belief was so unusual. It was because he seemed to believe it so strongly.

In general, Usher believed that plants could feel and know things. He also believed that *all* nonliving things had the same power. Usher saw evidence of this in the gray stones of his house. There were also signs in the plants that spread over the walls and the dying trees around the house. And, he added, there seemed to be a certain vapor that hung about the place. I shook in fear when he described this. It was the same feeling I had when I'd first set eyes on the mansion.

One evening Usher informed me suddenly that Lady Madeline had died. He stated that he would not bury her right away in the family burial place. Instead, he wanted to place her in one of the many vaults inside the main building. He said he was doing this mainly because the doctors had been very curious about her illness.

I saw no reason to oppose the plan. I remembered the unpleasant look on the doctor's face the day I arrived. I thought the idea made sense.

At Usher's request I helped him carry the body to a small, damp, dark vault. It was directly beneath that part of the house where my room was. At one time long ago, the vault had been a prison. In later days, it had been a storage place for gunpowder. Part of its floor and the long archway we had passed through were lined with copper. Copper also lined the vault's heavy iron door. It made a sharp grating sound as it moved on its hinges.

We set down our sad burden and lifted the lid of the coffin. We looked upon the face of Lady

Madeline. I was shocked to see how much she looked like her brother. Usher saw my surprise. He mumbled that he and Lady Madeline were twins. He said they were tied together in ways that no one could know.

We did not look long upon Lady Madeline. The faint blush that seemed to appear on her face even in death startled us. We replaced and screwed down the lid. Then we locked the door behind us. We made our way back to the rooms in the upper house. They were as gloomy as the room from which we'd come.

Several days of bitter grief passed. Then a change came over my friend. He roamed from room to room with a hurried and uneven step.

But there was no purpose to his movements. His face had grown even paler, and the brightness in his eyes had completely gone out. He spoke with a constant note of terror in his voice.

Sometimes I thought he had some terrible secret on his mind, and he was trying to find the courage to talk about it. At other times, I thought he acted like a madman. I would find him staring into space for hours, as if listening to a sound only he could hear. No wonder his behavior scared me. I kept thinking about his wild superstitions.

It was a week or so after Lady Madeline's death. I went to bed late that night, but I could not sleep. I tried for hours to fight off the nervous feeling I had. The dark curtains moved about in the breeze of a coming storm. Slowly my whole body began to shake. My heart felt a heavy weight of fear.

I lifted myself upon the pillows and stared into the darkness. I could hear low and mysterious sounds at times when the storm eased up. I got up quickly and threw on my clothes. I knew that I could no longer sleep that night. I tried to shake off my fear by walking back and forth across the room.

A few moments later I heard light footsteps on the stairs. I knew it was Usher. An instant later, he knocked gently at the door. Then he entered, carrying a lamp.

He looked deathly, as usual. And he was quite hysterical. Even so, having him there was better than being alone. I welcomed his presence as a relief.

"You have not seen it?" he asked after looking about the room. "You have not seen it? But stay, you will."

He rushed over to a window and opened it wide to the storm. The powerful gusts nearly lifted us from our feet. Thick clouds pressed down on the building. We had no glimpse of the moon or stars, nor was there any flash of lightning. But still, some of the objects on the ground below glowed in the strange light of the vapor that hung about the house.

"You must not look at this!" I said shuddering. I closed the window and dragged Usher over to a seat. "There is a mist rising from the lake. It is chilling and harmful to your health. Here is a book. I will read to you. And we will pass away this terrible night together."

I knew the book I had chosen would hold no interest for him. But it was the only one close by, and I was hoping that his mind would be eased by any reading. I had read several pages of the old story before I came to the following:

And Ethelred lifted his club against the door. Then with mighty blows he cracked and ripped and tore it all apart. And the noise sounded throughout the forest.

At the end of this section I leaned forward and paused for a moment. I thought I heard a sound coming from a distant part of the house. And in my excited state of mind, the sound appeared to be exactly like the one described in the book.

I continued with the story:

And Ethelred came through the door. Within he found a fiery dragon which sat on guard. Ethelred lifted up his club and struck the dragon upon the head. And the dragon fell before him with an awful cry. Ethelred was forced to hold his hands to his ears against the horrible noise.

I paused once more. I was amazed. Now I was sure I heard a low, harsh screaming or grating sound off in the distance. It sounded much like what I thought must have been the dragon's cry in the book.

As excited as I was, I was careful not to upset my friend. I was not certain that he had heard these sounds. Yet there had been, in the past few minutes, a change in his manner.

He had moved his chair around so he was facing the door of the room. I could see part of his face. His lips were trembling, as if he were whispering to himself. His head had dropped to his chest. Yet, I could tell he was not asleep because his eyes were wide open. His body rocked from side to side in a gentle sway.

After noticing all of this, I went on reading:

Now Ethelred removed the beast from out of his way. He went over the silver pavement of the castle to where the shield hung upon the wall. And the shield fell down at his feet with a terrible ringing sound.

No sooner had the words passed my lips than I heard a distant clanging sound. It was indeed as if a metal shield had fallen upon a floor of silver. I leaped to my feet in terror.

Usher continued his steady rocking movements. I rushed to his chair. His eyes were staring straight ahead, and his face was like stone. I placed my hand upon his shoulder, and his body shuddered. A sick smile came over his lips, and he spoke in a low, hurried murmur. He spoke as if I wasn't there. Bending near him, I finally understood the horrible meaning of his words.

"Yes, I hear it and *have* heard it. I have heard it for many minutes, many hours, many days. Yet, oh pity me, I *dared* not speak! Did I not tell you that my senses were sharp? I now tell you that I heard her first weak movements in the coffin. I heard them many, many days ago. Yet, I *dared* not speak! *We have put her living in the tomb!*

"And now tonight—Ethelred and the breaking of the door and the death-cry of the dragon. Then the clanging of the shield! Or rather, the breaking of her coffin and the grating of the iron door of her prison. And then her struggles within the copper archway of the vault!

"Oh, where shall I hide? Will she not be here soon? Is she not hurrying to blame me for my haste? For burying her alive? Have I not heard her footsteps on the stair?" Here he jumped to his feet and screamed out the words, *"I tell you that she now stands outside the door."*

Just then the huge door to the room opened slowly. It was the work of a gust of wind. Yet, outside the room did stand the ghostly figure of Lady Madeline. There was blood upon her white robes. And there were signs of some bitter struggle upon every part of her body.

For a moment she remained trembling. She rocked back and forth at the doorway. Then with a low, moaning cry she fell heavily in her final struggle with death. She fell upon her brother and carried him to the floor with her. He lay there dead, a victim of all he had feared.

I ran in terror from the room and the house. The storm was still in full fury as I crossed the old bridge. Suddenly I saw a wild light along the path. I turned to see where it had come from. The brightness was coming from the full, blood-red moon. It shone through the zigzag crack that ran down the front wall of the house.

While I looked, the crack quickly widened. Then a strong gust of wind came forth. My mind was spinning as I watched the walls break apart. There was a sound like the rush of a thousand waters. And then the deep and dark lake at my feet closed silently over the House of Usher.

The Oval Portrait

My servant insisted that because of my wounded condition we could not spend the night in the open air. So he took it upon himself to break into the castle we had come across in the Italian mountains. The building was a mixture of gloom and splendor. It seemed to have been abandoned, at least for the time being.

We set ourselves up in one of the smallest furnished rooms. It lay in a distant part of the building. The room's decorations were expensive, but old and worn. On its walls hung curtains and shelves that held many trophies. In addition, there were a great number of lively modern paintings in rich gold frames.

These paintings hung not only from the walls. They were also present in the many corners of this odd-shaped building. I don't know why— perhaps it was due to my confused state because of my wound—but I began to take a deep interest in these paintings.

I asked my servant, Pedro, to close the heavy shutters of the room. And since it was already night, I asked him to light the candles of a tall candelabrum that was at the head of the bed.

Finally, I told him to throw open the black velvet curtains that surrounded the bed itself.

I wanted all this done so that if I couldn't sleep, at least I could look at these many pictures. At the same time, I could read a small book I had found that described them.

I read for a long time. And I gazed with pleasure at the paintings for just as long. The hours flew by, and it was soon midnight. The position of the candelabrum bothered me. Not wishing to disturb my sleeping servant, I moved it myself. I did this so there would be better light for me to read. However, this movement produced another effect.

The light from the candelabrum now fell within a part of the room that had been hidden before. I now saw in bright light a picture I had not yet noticed.

It was a portrait of a young girl close to womanhood. I glanced at the painting quickly and then closed my eyes. I wasn't sure at first why I did this. But while my lids were closed, I ran over in my mind my reason for shutting them.

I needed time to think. I wanted to make sure my eyes had not fooled me. I needed to calm my mind for a more certain look. In a few moments I gazed once more at the painting.

As I have already said, it was a portrait of a young girl. It showed just the head and shoulders, done in what is usually called a *vignette*. The arms, bosom, even the ends of the glowing hair, melted into the deep shadow of the painting's background. The frame was oval and done in a beautiful design.

As art, nothing could have been more worthy of praise. But it was neither the work of the artist, nor the everlasting beauty of the young woman, which had so moved me. I thought seriously about these points. I stayed for an hour, perhaps, with my eyes glued to the portrait. Finally I was satisfied with the true secret of its effect.

The spell of the picture was how real, how *life-like* it was. It confused and horrified me. In deep fear I put the candelabrum back in its earlier position. The cause of my fear was now shut from view. I eagerly picked up the book that discussed the paintings and their histories. I turned to the page which listed the oval portrait. I then read the charming and somewhat unclear words that follow:

"She was a young woman of rare beauty, and as happy as she was lovely. And evil was the hour when she saw, and loved, and married the painter. He was serious, full of passion, and already married to his Art. The beautiful young woman was happy and held all things dear. She hated only the Art which was her rival.

"So it was a terrible thing for this lady to hear the painter speak of his wish to portray her, his bride. But she was humble and obeyed him. She sat quietly for many weeks in the dark high tower. The light dripped upon the pale canvas only from overhead.

"But the painter took glory in his work. And it went on from hour to hour and from day to day. He was a wild and moody man, and he became lost in his work. He *would* not see that the light that fell so grimly within the room damaged the health of his bride.

"Yet she smiled on and did not complain, because she saw that the painter, a famous man, took a burning pleasure in his job. And he worked hard day and night to portray the one who loved him so. Yet day by day she grew more unhappy and weak.

"Some who saw the painting spoke of it as proof of the deep love the painter held for his bride. But as the work was nearly finished, no one was allowed into the tower. The painter had grown wild in his love for his work. He rarely turned his eyes from the canvas to look at the face of his wife. And he *would* not see that the color which he spread upon the canvas was drawn from her cheeks.

"Many weeks passed, and there was little left to do. There was one brush to place upon the mouth, and one tint upon the eye. And the brush was given, and the tint was placed. Then for one moment the painter stood spellbound before the work he had created.

"In the next moment while he stared, he grew shaky and pale. He cried out in a loud voice, 'This is indeed *Life* itself!' And when he turned to look at his beloved—*she was dead*."

The Masque of the Red Death

The "Red Death" had long been destroying the country. No disease had ever been so deadly or so terrible. Blood was the form it chose. Its mark was the redness and the horror of blood.

Its victims suffered sharp pains and sudden dizziness. There was heavy bleeding at the pores and then death. This resulted in bright red stains upon the body, and especially on the face. It caused the victim to be shut away from the help and sympathy of others. The disease took only about a half hour to strike and kill.

But Prince Prospero was happy, daring, and wise. When half of his people had died, he sent for a thousand healthy and light-hearted friends. He chose these people from among the knights and ladies of his court. Then he and his friends retired behind the walls of one of his castles.

The building was large and magnificent. A strong, high wall surrounded it. This wall had gates of iron. The servants brought furnaces and hammers and welded shut the bolts of the gate. There was to be no entrance or exit from the castle for whatever reason.

The outside world could take care of itself. In the meantime, it was foolish to grieve or to think. The prince had provided all the means of pleasure. There were clowns, ballet dancers, and musicians. There was plenty of food, and there was wine. All this and security remained inside. Outside was the "Red Death."

The prince and his thousand friends stayed in seclusion for the next six months. All the while the disease spread throughout the land. Then the prince decided to hold a masked ball of the most unusual kind.

It was a great and wonderful affair. But first let me tell of the rooms in which it was held. There were seven—a royal suite. In many palaces such suites form a long and straight line. The folding doors slide back nearly to the walls on either side. This way the view of the whole suite is hardly blocked.

Here the case was very different, as might have been expected from the prince's love of the *bizarre*. The suite was set up so oddly that one could barely see more than one room at a time. There was a sharp turn at every 20 or 30 yards. And at each turn there was a different effect.

To the right and left, in the middle of each wall, was a tall and narrow window. This window looked out upon a closed hallway that followed the turns of the suite. These windows were made of stained glass. The color of the glass matched the decorations of the room into which the window opened.

For example, the room at the eastern end had blue decorations. And its windows were a deep blue. The second room had purple ornaments and tapestries. And here the panes were purple. The third room was green throughout—and so were the windows. The fourth room was furnished and lighted with orange—the fifth with white—the sixth with violet.

The seventh room was closely covered in black velvet tapestries. They hung all over the ceiling and down the walls. They fell in heavy folds upon a carpet of the same material and color. But in this room only, the color of the windows failed to match the decorations. The panes here were scarlet—a deep blood-red color.

In not one of the seven rooms was there any lamp or candelabrum. In fact there was no light of any kind coming from within the suite. But in the hallways, opposite each window, stood a table. On this table was a metal container with a flame that reflected off the tinted glass and lit up the room.

This light produced many fantastic sights. But the effect in the black room was different. The firelight that streamed in upon the dark curtains and the blood-tinted panes was horrible. It produced a wild look on the faces of all those who entered. And there were few in the company bold enough to set foot inside the room at all.

In this room, there was also a huge, ebony clock. Its pendulum swung back and forth with a dull, heavy clang. And each hour there came from the clock a clear, loud, deep sound. The sound was so unusual that each hour the orchestra was forced to pause to listen to it. The waltzers, too, stopped their dancing, and the entire happy crowd was upset for a moment.

However, when the sound stopped, a light laughter once again filled the room. The musicians looked at each other and smiled, as if at their own foolishness. And they made whispering vows to each other that the next time the clock chimed they would not stop playing. Yet, when another hour had passed and the clock chimed, the same uneasiness was felt by all.

In spite of these things, it was a merry and magnificent affair. The tastes of the prince were strange. He had a fine eye for color and effect. He ignored the normal rules of fashion. His plans were bold and fiery. There were some who would have thought him mad. Yet, his followers felt he was not.

He had chosen, in large part, the colors and decorations of the seven rooms for this great party. And it was his own taste that had set the tone for the masqueraders. To be sure, the costumes were strange or ugly. There was much glare and glitter—and much that was unreal.

There were strange figures with unusual legs and arms. There were wild designs. There was much of the beautiful, and much of the *bizarre*. There was something of the terrible, and something of that which might cause disgust.

Back and forth in the seven rooms stalked the many masqueraders—appearing as if they were dreams. These "dreams" twisted in and about, taking color from the rooms. And they caused the wild music of the orchestra to seem like the echo of their steps.

Then the ebony clock struck. For a moment all was still and silent except the voice of the clock. The dreams seemed frozen as they stood. But the echoes of the sound died away. They had lasted only for an instant. And a light, quiet laughter floated after them. Then the music swelled, and the dreams came to life again, twisting and turning more merrily than ever.

But to the most westward room—the black room—none of the maskers had gone. For there, through the blood-colored panes, flowed a deep mysterious light. And the blackness of the drapes added to the terrifying effect.

The other rooms were very crowded, and in them beat the heart of life. The party went gaily on, until finally the clock struck midnight. Then the music stopped, as I have told. The dancing of the waltzers was halted. And there was an uneasy quietness as before.

Now there were 12 strokes of the clock to be sounded. Perhaps with more time, more thought crept into the minds of the crowd. And perhaps, too, before the final chime had sounded, many in the crowd had become aware of a certain masked figure. This figure had not drawn the attention of anyone before. Now the rumor of his presence was spreading. And there arose a murmur of disapproval and surprise. These feelings turned finally to ones of terror and disgust.

It may be thought that among this strange crowd no such costume could have caused such a feeling. In truth, the nature of the costumes that night knew no limits. But the figure in question had gone even beyond the prince's tastes. The whole company seemed to feel that the costume and manner of the stranger was neither amusing nor proper.

The figure was tall and thin. And it was covered from head to foot in the clothing of the grave. The mask that covered the face was made to resemble the face of a stiffened corpse. And all of this might still have been accepted by the masqueraders. But this figure had gone so far as to assume the look of the Red Death. His clothing was dabbed in *blood*. And his entire face was sprinkled with the red horror.

When Prince Prospero first set eyes upon this image, he began to shake violently. Then, in the next moment, his brow reddened with rage.

"Who dares?" he demanded of the servants who stood near him. "Who dares insult us this way? Seize him and unmask him. That way we may know whom we have to hang at sunrise!"

Prince Prospero was in the eastern, or blue, room when he spoke these words. But they rang throughout the seven rooms loudly and clearly. For the prince was a bold and healthy man. And the music had become hushed at the waving of his hand.

At first, the prince's servants made a slight rushing movement toward the figure, who was coming closer to the speaker. But the figure had inspired great fear among the crowd. So no one put out a hand to stop him. Without trouble, he passed within a yard of the prince.

Then the huge crowd shrank back from the centers of the rooms toward the walls. And the figure made his way, without interruption,

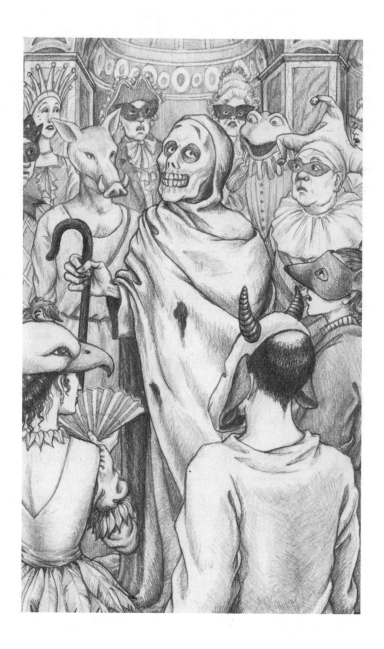

through the rooms. He walked with steady steps from the blue room to the purple. Then he moved from the purple to the green—through the green to the orange. He made his way through the orange to the white and from there to the violet.

It was then, however, that Prince Prospero rushed through the six rooms. He was mad with rage and filled with shame at his own lack of courage. But no one followed him because a deadly terror had seized all.

The prince held above him a drawn dagger. He approached to within three or four feet of the figure. Then the figure, having reached the entrance of the black room, turned suddenly to face him.

There was a sharp cry—and the dagger dropped shining upon the sable carpet. An instant later Prince Prospero fell face downward in death.

Then, gathering a wild courage, a group of masqueraders ran into the black room. There they seized the figure, who stood tall and straight within the shadow of the clock. There was a gasp of horror. For the clothing and corpse-like mask, which they had so violently grabbed, was empty of any physical form.

Now the presence of the Red Death was recognized. He had come like a thief in the night.

One by one the partygoers dropped in the blood-stained halls of their party. The life of the ebony clock went out with the last of the masqueraders. And the flames outside the colored windows went out as well. Darkness and Decay and the Red Death ruled over all.

The Tell-Tale Heart

Nervous—very, very nervous I had been and am. But why do you say that I am mad? The disease had sharpened my senses—not destroyed or dulled them. Especially sharp was the sense of hearing. I heard all things in heaven and on earth. I heard many things in hell. How, then, am I mad? Listen! And see how clearly and calmly I can tell you the whole story.

It is impossible to say how the idea first entered my brain. But once it was born, it haunted me day and night. There was no reason for it. There was no passion to it. I loved the old man. He had never wronged me. He had never insulted me. I had no desire for his gold.

I think it was his eye! Yes, it was this! He had the eye of a vulture. It was a pale blue eye with a film over it. Whenever it looked at me, my blood ran cold. And so very gradually I made up my mind to take the life of the old man. This way I would be rid of the eye forever.

Now this is the point. You think I am mad. Madmen know nothing. But you should have seen *me*. You should have seen how wisely, how carefully I went to work. I was never kinder to the old man than during the whole week before I killed him. Every night, about midnight, I turned the latch of his door. And I opened it—oh so gently.

The opening I made was large enough for my head. I put in a dark lantern, all closed, so that no light shone out. Then I thrust in my head. You would have laughed to see how smartly I thrust it in! I moved it very, very slowly so that I might not disturb the old man's sleep. Ha!—Would a madman have been so wise as this?

Then, when I was in the room, I undid the lantern carefully—oh, so carefully. I undid it just enough so that a single thin ray fell upon the vulture eye. This I did for seven long nights— every night just at midnight. But I found the eye always closed. So it was impossible to do the work. For it was not the old man that annoyed me, but his Evil Eye.

Every morning, when day broke, I went boldly into his room. And I spoke bravely to him. I called him by his first name in a friendly tone and asked how he had passed the night. So he would have been a very smart man indeed to suspect what I did every night at midnight.

On the eighth night I was more careful than ever in opening the door. Never before that night had I *felt* the strength of my powers—of my wisdom. I could hardly hold in my feelings of triumph. There I had been opening the door little by little each night. And he did not even dream of my secret deeds or thoughts.

I almost laughed at the idea, and perhaps he heard me. For he moved on the bed suddenly, as if he were startled. Now you may think that I drew back—but no. His room was pitch black, for the shutters were closed. So I knew he could not see the opening of the door. I kept pushing it open steadily, steadily.

I had my head in. I was about to open the lantern, when my thumb slipped on the tin fastening. The old man sprang up in the bed and cried out, "Who's there?"

I kept quite still and said nothing. For a whole hour I did not move a muscle. And during that hour I did not hear him lie down. He was sitting up in the bed listening.

Soon, I heard a slight groan. It was not a groan of pain or of grief. Oh, no! It was the low, muffled sound that comes up from the soul when it is filled with fear.

I knew the sound well. Many a night, just at midnight, it had welled up from my own chest. And with its awful echo, it deepened the terrors that disturbed me. I knew what the old man felt, and I pitied him, although I chuckled at heart.

I waited a long time without hearing him lie down. I decided to make a slight opening in the lantern. I did so quietly—you cannot imagine how quietly. Finally, a single dim ray shot out from the opening and fell upon the vulture eye.

The eye was open, wide open. And I grew furious as I gazed upon it. I saw it perfectly. It was a dull blue, with a disgusting veil over it that chilled my very bones. But I could see nothing else of the old man's body. For I had directed the light right upon the spot.

I have told you that what you mistake for madness is a sharpness of my senses. Now I say that what came to my ears was a low, dull, quick sound. It was a sound such as a watch makes when it is covered with cotton. I knew *that* sound well, too. It was the beating of the old man's heart. It increased my fury, as the beating of the drum stirs the soldier's courage.

Yet, I kept still. I hardly breathed. I did not move the lantern. I tried to hold the ray of light steadily upon the eye. Meantime the horrible beating of the heart continued. It grew quicker and quicker, and louder and louder. The old man's terror *must* have been rather intense.

It grew louder, I say, louder every moment! Do you hear me? I told you that I am nervous. So I am. Now at this dead hour of the night, in the awful silence of that old house, this strange noise excited me to great terror. The beating grew louder, louder! I thought the heart would burst.

Now a new worry seized me. The sound would soon be heard by a neighbor! The old man's hour had come. With a loud yell, I threw open the lantern and jumped into the room.

He cried out once—only once. In an instant I dragged him to the floor and pulled the heavy bed over him. I then smiled happily to find the deed done. But for many minutes the heart beat on with a muffled sound. This, however, did not bother me. It would not be heard through the wall. Finally it stopped. The old man was dead.

I removed the bed and examined the corpse. Yes, he was stone dead. I placed my hand upon the heart and held it there for many minutes. There was no pulse. He was dead. His eye would trouble me no more.

Do you still think me mad? You will think so no longer when I describe how I hid the body. I worked quickly, but in silence. I took up three planks from the floor. Then I placed the body under the boards and replaced them. I did this so cleverly that no human eye—not even *his*— could have found anything wrong.

When I had finished it was four o'clock, still dark as midnight. There came a knocking at the street door. I went down to open it with a light heart. For what had I *now* to fear?

Three men entered. They introduced themselves as officers of the police. A cry had

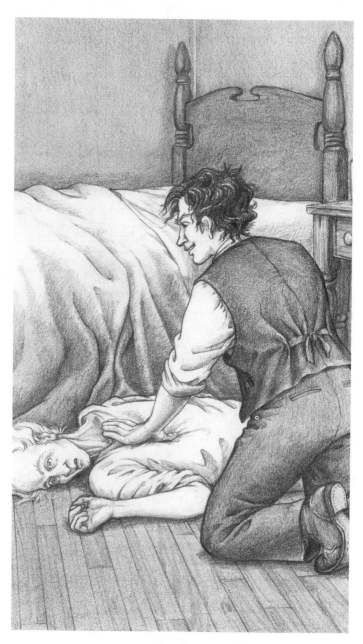

36

been heard by a neighbor during the night. Someone suspected foul play. The police had been called, and these men were ordered to search the house.

I smiled, for *what* had I to fear? The cry, I said, was my own in a dream. The old man, I said, was away in the country. I took my visitors all over the house. I told them to search—search *well*.

Finally, I led them to *his* room. I showed them his treasures, safe and secure. I brought chairs into the room and told them to rest *here*. And I placed myself in a chair above the very spot where the victim was buried!

The officers were satisfied. I was at ease. They sat and talked of familiar things. But before long, I felt myself getting pale and wished them gone. My head ached, and I thought I heard a ringing in my ears. The ringing became clearer. I talked more freely to get rid of the sound. But it continued. Finally, I found that the noise was *not* within my ears.

The sound increased—and what could I do? It was *a low, dull quick sound, much like a watch makes when it is covered with cotton.* I gasped for breath—yet the officers did not hear it. I talked more quickly, more forcefully. But the noise steadily increased.

I paced the floor with heavy strides. But the noise steadily increased. Oh, God! What could I do? I swung the chair upon which I had been sitting and scraped it upon the boards. But the noise continued.

It grew louder—louder—*louder!* And still the men talked pleasantly. Was it possible they did not hear it? No! They heard. They suspected. They *knew*. They were making a fool of me.

Anything was better than this agony! I could bear those awful smiles no longer. I felt I must scream or die! And now again, listen! louder! louder! *louder!*

"Villains!" I cried. "Search no more! I admit the deed. Tear up the planks! Here—here! It is the beating of his awful heart!"

The Pit and
the Pendulum

I was sick—sick unto death with that long agony. Finally they untied me, and I was allowed to sit. Then I felt that my senses were leaving me. The sentence—the dreaded sentence of death—was the last clear sound which reached my ears.

After that, the voices of the judges seemed to come together in one dreamy hum. This was only for a brief period, for soon I heard no more. Yet, for a while, I saw. But what a sight! I saw the lips of the black-robed judges. They appeared to me white—whiter than the paper upon which I write these words. And the lips were thin—with a grim firmness.

I saw that the words of my fate were still coming from those lips. I saw them say the syllables of my name. And I shuddered because I heard no sound. And then my vision fell upon the seven tall candles upon the table. At first they seemed like slim white angels who would save me. Then a deadly sickness came over me. And the candles seemed like ghosts with heads of flame that would be of no help.

Suddenly a thought came to me, like a rich musical note. What sweet rest there must be in the grave. The thought came gently and quietly. But just as my spirit came to accept it, the figures of the judges disappeared, as if by magic. The tall candles sank into nothingness and their flames went out completely. Then silence, and stillness, and night were my world.

I swooned, but I will not say that I passed out. I was not entirely awake, nor entirely unconscious. Shadows of memory tell me of tall figures that lifted and carried me in silence down to a great depth. They also tell of a horrible feeling in my heart—an unnatural stillness. After this I remember a flatness and dampness. And then all is *madness*—the madness of a memory that wishes to forget forbidden things.

Suddenly movement and sound came rushing back to me. It was the movement of the heart, and in my ears the sound of its beating. Then there was a pause in which all was blank. Then again sound, movement, and touch—a tingling feeling throughout my body. Then suddenly *thought*—and terror—and a great effort to understand my true state. Finally there was full memory of the trial. There was memory of the judges, of the sentence, of the sickness, and of the swoon.

So far, I had not opened my eyes. I felt that I was lying upon my back, untied. I reached out my hand, and it fell upon something damp and hard. I remained that way for many minutes. I tried to imagine where I could be.

I longed to, but dared not, use my eyes. I dreaded that first glance at the objects around me. It was not that I was afraid to look upon horrible things. I was afraid that there would be *nothing* to see. Finally, with a desperate heart, I quickly opened my eyes.

My worst thoughts came true. The blackness of night surrounded me. I struggled for breath. I still lay quietly and tried to think. I thought once more of the judges. I tried to figure out my real condition.

The sentence had been passed. It seemed to me that a very long period of time had since gone by. Yet not for a moment did I think I was actually dead. But where and in what state was I? Had I been taken back to my dungeon to await execution? Yet that could not be. My dungeon, like all the cells of the condemned at Toledo, had stone floors and small windows to let in some light.

A horrible idea suddenly caused the blood to rush upon my heart. For a brief period I lost all my senses again. When I recovered, I jumped to my feet, shaking all over. I thrust my arms wildly above and around me in all directions. I felt nothing, yet I dreaded to move a step. I was afraid I would feel the walls of a *tomb*.

Large cold beads of sweat burst out upon my forehead. I could no longer stand the suspense. I moved forward slowly with my arms in front of me. My eyes strained in the hope of catching some small ray of light. I walked several paces, but still all was empty and black. I breathed a bit easier. It seemed clear that mine was not, at least, the most horrible of fates.

I continued to step carefully onward. Now my mind recalled a thousand rumors of the horrors of Toledo. Of the dungeons there had been strange tales told. I had always believed them to be fables. Yet they were strange and too horrible to repeat except in a whisper.

Was I left to die of starvation in this underground world of darkness? Or, what fate, perhaps even more fearful, awaited me? The result I knew would be death, and a bitter one. I knew my judges too well to doubt that. The method and the hour were all that were unknown to me.

My outstretched hands finally came upon a wall. It was made of stone—very smooth, slimy, and cold. I followed it carefully. But this gave me no way of figuring out the total space of my dungeon. I might cover the entire area and return to where I set out without knowing it.

So I looked for the knife that had been in my pocket when I was led before the Court. But it was gone. My clothes had been replaced by a robe of coarse material. I had wanted to force the knife into some crack in the wall to mark where I had started from.

Instead, I tore off a piece of cloth from my robe. Then I placed it against the wall. I would have to come across this rag when I had made a complete trip around the cell.

So, at least, I thought. But I had not counted upon the size of the dungeon, or my own weakness. The ground was damp and slippery. I staggered on for some time, when I stumbled and fell. I was so tired that I was forced to stay where I fell. And sleep soon overtook me.

When I woke up, I stretched out my arm and found a loaf of bread and a pitcher of water beside me. I didn't even think about it. I just ate and drank as fast as I could.

A bit later I continued my walk around the dungeon. After a while I finally came upon the cloth I had placed near the wall. Up until my fall, I had counted 52 steps. Now I counted another 48 steps until I reached the rag.

There were then 100 steps in all. Figuring two steps for each yard, I figured the dungeon to be about 50 yards around. However, I had come across many angles in the wall. So, I couldn't guess the shape of the vault.

There was no hope in learning more about my dungeon. But I was still curious, and that made me continue. I moved away from the wall and decided to cross the area of the cell. At first I moved very carefully. For the floor, which seemed solid, was covered with slime. Finally, I found my courage and began to step firmly.

I tried to walk in as straight a line as possible. I advanced about 10 or 12 steps forward. Then the piece of cloth I had torn from my robe became tangled between my legs. I stepped on it and fell down hard on my face.

When I fell, I was at first confused. I did not understand the situation. A few seconds later, while I still lay face down, I became aware of it.

It was this—my chin rested upon the floor of the prison. But my lips and the upper part of my head, although lower than the chin, touched nothing. At the same time my forehead seemed bathed in a damp vapor.

I put my arms forward. I found that I had fallen at the very edge of a circular pit. Of course, I had no way of knowing how deep or wide this pit was. I felt below the edge and pulled a small stone loose. Then I let it fall into the pit.

For many seconds it bounced off the sides before it finally plunged into the water. Just then I heard a sound from above. It sounded like a quick opening and closing of a door overhead. At the same moment a faint light flashed through the gloom. Then just as suddenly it faded away.

I saw clearly the doom which had been prepared for me. I was grateful for the timely accident that had helped me escape it. Another step, and the world would not have seen me again. I had been given a choice of death. I could have a sudden death by dropping into the pit or die a slower, more horrible death.

Shaking all over, I felt my way back to the wall. I made up my mind to die there rather than risk the terrors of the pit. In another state of mind, I might have decided to end it all at once. But now I was a coward. And I could not forget what I had read of these pits. *Sudden* death was not part of the horrible plan behind them.

I remained awake for many long hours, but finally I fell asleep again. When I awoke, I found by my side, as before, a loaf of bread and a pitcher of water. I felt a burning thirst, so I quickly emptied the pitcher. It must have been drugged, for I felt very sleepy at once.

A deep sleep fell upon me. How long it lasted I do not know. But when I opened my eyes again, I could see the objects around me. There was also a strange glow. I could not figure out where it came from at first.

I had been greatly mistaken about the size of my prison. It was not more than 25 yards around. The reason for my mistake finally flashed upon me. I had at first counted 52 steps up to the time when I fell. I then must have been within a step or two of the piece of cloth. In fact I had nearly completed a trip around the entire vault. I then slept. Upon waking I must have repeated the same steps. So I had supposed the trip around was nearly double what it really was.

I had been fooled too, in regard to the shape of the dungeon. In feeling my way around, I had found many angles. So I thought the shape of the place was quite unusual. The effect of total darkness upon someone just waking up is very strong. The angles were just slight grooves. The general shape of the prison was square.

I was also mistaken about the walls. What I had taken to be stone was actually iron, or some other metal, in huge plates. On the walls were crudely painted pictures of devils in skeleton forms and scary poses. In the center of the prison was the round pit from which I had escaped.

All this I saw with much effort. For my condition had greatly changed while I was asleep. I now lay upon my back, stretched out, on a low wooden framework. I was tied tightly to it by a long strap. It passed around and around my limbs and body.

Only my head and left arm were somewhat free. This allowed me, with great effort, to take some food from a dish that lay beside me. I saw, to my horror, that the pitcher of water had been removed. I say to my horror, because I was very thirsty. The cause of this appeared to be the salty meat in the dish. And it was clear that my persecutors had planned this.

Looking upward, I saw the ceiling of my prison. It was some 30 or 40 feet overhead. It was built much as the side walls were. In one of its panels a figure caught my attention. It was the painted figure of Time, as he is usually seen. Except he was not holding a scythe. Instead he held what appeared to be a huge pendulum, such as we see on old clocks.

There was something about the pendulum that caused me to look at it more closely. When I gazed directly up at it, I thought I saw it move. A moment later, I *knew* that it had moved. Its sweep was brief and slow. I watched it for some minutes in wonder. Finally, I got tired of its dull movements. I turned my attention to the other objects in the cell.

A slight noise caught my attention. Looking at the floor, I noticed several huge rats running about. They had come from the well, which lay just within view to my right. Even as I watched, they came up in large numbers. They were drawn by the smell of the meat. I finally managed to scare them away.

A half hour, or perhaps even an hour, went by. Then once again I looked upward. What I saw amazed me. The sweep of the pendulum had increased by almost a yard. As a natural result, its speed was also much greater. But what mainly disturbed me was the idea that it was noticeably *lower*.

I now saw—in horror—that its lower part was a curved edge made of glittering steel. This part was about a foot in length from tip to tip. The ends tapered and pointed upward, and the edge seemed as sharp as a razor. It appeared heavy and was attached to a thick rod of brass. The whole thing *hissed* as it swung through the air.

I no longer wondered about the doom prepared for me. My discovery of the pit had become known to my persecutors. The horrors of the *pit* had been saved for someone, like myself, who so boldly disobeyed them. The *pit* was rumored to be the most horrible of all their punishments.

I had avoided falling into the pit by a simple accident. I knew that surprise was an important part of the plan. Having failed to fall in on my own, there was no plan to throw me in. Therefore, a different and milder form of death was in store for me. Milder! I half smiled in my agony as I thought of using such a word.

Why bother to tell of the long, long hours of horror that followed. I counted the rushing vibrations of the steel—inch by inch, line by line. Days passed. It might have been that many days passed. The pendulum swept so close to me that I felt it fan me with its movement. The smell of the sharp steel forced itself into my nose.

I prayed, prayed for its more speedy descent. I grew mad. I struggled to force myself upward

against the sweep of the fearful blade. And then I fell suddenly calm. I lay smiling at the glittering death, as a child at some rare toy.

There was another period of passing out. It might have been brief. For when I came to, there had been no further drop of the pendulum. Then again, it might have been long. I knew there were demons who took note of my condition. They could have stopped the pendulum at their pleasure while I was asleep.

I felt sick and weak. It felt as though I had gone without eating for a long time. With a painful effort, I reached out with my left arm as far as I could. I found a piece of food that had been spared by the rats.

I put the food to my lips. And a half-formed thought rushed to my mind. It was a thought of joy—of hope. Yet what business had *I* with hope? It was, as I say, a half-formed thought. Suddenly it faded. I struggled to bring it back. My long suffering had almost destroyed my ordinary powers of mind.

The sweep of the pendulum was at right angles to my body. I saw that the blade was set to cross the area of my heart. It would touch the very edges of my robe. Then it would return to repeat the movement again and again. This fraying of my robe would be all that it would do for several minutes.

I concentrated hard on this thought. It was as if by so doing, I could stop *here* the descent of the steel. I forced myself to think about the sound the pendulum would make as it passed across the robe. I thought about this until my teeth were on edge.

Down—down it came. To the right—to the left—far and wide it swept. Down to my heart it came with the steady pace of a tiger. I laughed and howled wildly.

Down it continued to come. It swept to within three inches of my chest. I struggled violently to free my left arm. It was free only from the elbow to the hand. If only I could have broken the bands above the elbow. I would have grabbed and tried to stop the pendulum. I might as well have tried to stop an avalanche!

Still further down it came. I gasped and struggled at each movement. Although death would have been a relief, oh, how unspeakable!

I saw that ten or twelve sweeps would bring the steel in contact with my robe. When I noticed this, my spirit was suddenly filled with a calmness. For the first time during many hours—perhaps days—I *thought.*

It now came to me that the band that held me down was all one piece. The first stroke of the blade on any part of the band would break it. Then, it might be unwound from my body with my left hand. But how fearfully close the blade would be! The smallest movement upward of my body would be deadly!

Was it possible that my persecutors had not thought of this? Was it possible that the band crossed my chest in the track of the pendulum? I lifted my head to view my breast. The band passed over my limbs and body in all directions—*except in the path of the pendulum!*

I dropped my head back again. Then, into my mind flashed the rest of the half-formed thought I mentioned earlier. The whole thought was now present. It was weak, hardly sane, hardly clear—but still whole.

For many hours the area around which I lay had been swarming with rats. They were wild, bold, and starving. Their red eyes glared at me. They were waiting for me to lie still so that they could make me their prey. "To what food have they been used to in the well?" I wondered.

They had already eaten all but a little of the food in the dish. I had waved my hand about the dish to move them away. After a while, it no longer had an effect. Their hunger forced them to sink their sharp fangs in my fingers. I grabbed whatever was left of the food. And I rubbed it into the band around me wherever I could reach it. Then I lay as still as I could.

At first the starving rats were startled at the change. Many shrank back. Some went down into the well. But this was only for a moment. I knew their hunger would bring them back.

One or two of them jumped upon the framework and smelled the band. That seemed to be a signal for a general rush. Fresh troops hurried up from the well. They clung to the wood. They overran it and leaped in hundreds upon my body.

The steady movement of the pendulum didn't disturb them at all. They avoided its strokes and busied themselves with the band. They swarmed upon me in greater and greater numbers. They covered my throat. Their cold lips touched mine. Disgust chilled my heart.

In a minute I felt the struggle would be over. I could plainly feel the loosening of the band. I knew that in more than one place it must already be cut. I struggled to keep still.

Finally, I felt that I was *free*. The band hung in pieces from my body. But the stroke of the pendulum already pressed upon my chest. Twice again it swung. A sharp pain shot through every nerve. But the moment of escape had arrived.

At a wave of my hand the rats hurried away. I moved carefully, sideways and slowly, out of the bonds. I was beyond the reach of the blade. For the moment, at least, I was *free!*

Free!—but in the grasp of the Inquisition! I took a small step from my bed of horror. Then the movement of the hellish machine stopped. I watched as it was pulled up, by an invisible force, through the ceiling. This was a sign I took to heart. My every move was being watched. I had escaped death by one form of torture only to suffer a worse death by another.

With that thought I rolled my eyes to the iron walls that closed me in. Some change, which I

could not at first figure out, had taken place. For many minutes I was in a dreamy state trying to guess what had happened.

During this time I learned where the dim glow that lighted the cell was coming from. It came from a crack, about a half inch wide. This crack ran around the entire prison at the base of the walls. These walls appeared to be entirely separated from the floor. I struggled, without success, to look through the opening.

As I got up, I at once solved the mystery of the change in the cell. I have already mentioned the pictures painted on the walls. Before, the colors had seemed blurred and unclear. Now these colors were very sharp and bright. Demon eyes, of a wild and awful nature, glared at me from every direction.

What now? I began to smell the odor of hot iron. I gasped for breath! There was no doubt about the plan of my persecutors. I shrank from the glowing metal to the center of the cell.

I thought of the fiery death that was in store for me. The idea of the coolness of the well calmed my soul. I rushed to its deadly edge. I strained my eyes to look below. The glare from the glowing roof lighted it to its deepest part. Yet, for a moment my mind did not understand what it saw. Finally, it forced itself into my soul.

Oh horror—any horror but this! I rushed from the edge and buried my face in my hands, weeping bitterly.

The heat quickly increased. Once again I looked up, shaking as if I had a fever. There had been a second change in the cell. This time the change was in the *form*. My attempts to escape had hurried my torturers. There was to be no more delay.

The room had once been square. Now the cell continued to change shape quickly with a low rumbling sound. Suddenly it became shaped like a diamond. But the change did not stop here. And I neither hoped nor wished it to stop.

"Death," I said, "any death but that of the pit." Fool! I might have known that the object of the burning iron was to urge me *into the pit.* Could I bear the heat? Could I bear the pressure? And now, flatter and flatter grew the cell. It was happening so quickly, I had no time to think.

Its center, its greatest width, was just over the terrible opening. I shrank back. But the closing walls pressed me onward. Finally, there was no longer an inch of foothold on the prison floor. I struggled no more. But the pain of my soul was set free in one loud, long final scream. I felt that I was on the edge. I turned my eyes away—

There was a strange hum of human voices. There was a loud blast of many trumpets. There was a constant booming of a thousand thunders. The fiery walls rushed back!

An outstretched arm caught my own as I fell into the well. It was the arm of General Lasalle. The French army had entered Toledo. The Inquisition was in the hands of its enemies. I was saved.

The Black Cat

I do not expect you to believe the wild tale I am about to write. I would have to be mad to expect it. Yet, mad I am not. And surely I do not dream. But tomorrow I die, and today I would like to cleanse my soul.

My purpose now is to place before the world a series of simple household events. These events have terrified, tortured, and destroyed me. Yet I will not try to explain them. Later, perhaps, someone smarter and calmer than I can do that. And that person will see in these events the natural result of causes and effects.

From my very early years, I was known for my gentle and pleasant nature. I was especially fond of animals. My parents supplied me with many different kinds of pets. I spent much time with them and was happiest when I was feeding and petting them. My love for animals continued as I grew up.

I married young. And I was happy to find that my wife had a similar nature to my own. When she saw my liking for household pets, she wasted no time getting us some. We had birds, goldfish, a fine dog, rabbits, a small monkey, and a *cat*.

The cat was a very large and beautiful black one. And he was wise to an amazing degree. When speaking of his intelligence, my wife often mentioned an old popular belief. This belief held that all black cats were witches in disguise. She was never *serious* about this point, however. I mention this only because I happen to remember it just now.

The cat's name was Pluto. He was my favorite pet. I alone fed him. And he followed me wherever I went around the house. He often even tried to follow me when I left the house.

Our friendship lasted this way for several years. During this time, however, my general nature was changing for the worse. The cause of this (I hate to admit) was due to the use of strong drink. Day by day I grew more moody. I cared less and less about the feelings of others. I began to use foul language to my wife and sometimes even struck her.

My pets, of course, began to feel the change in me. I not only neglected them, but treated them badly. Pluto was an exception. I still had enough feeling for him so as not to mistreat him. But nothing stopped me from mistreating the others when they got in my way.

However, my disease grew worse. For what disease is like alcohol! Finally, even Pluto began to feel the effects of my bad temper.

One night I returned home very drunk. When I thought that the cat was avoiding me, I grabbed him. He became frightened and gave me a slight wound upon my hand with his teeth.

The fury of a demon suddenly came over me. I no longer knew myself. My original soul seemed, at once, to leave my body. The evil effects of alcohol filled every bone in me. I took from my coat pocket a penknife and opened it. I grabbed the beast by the throat and cut one of its eyes from the socket! I shudder as I describe this horrible crime.

My reason returned in the morning when I had slept off the night's drink. I experienced both horror and sorrow for what I had done. But it was at best a weak, mixed feeling, and I remained unchanged. Once again I plunged into drinking, and the memory of the deed became drowned in wine.

In the meantime, the cat slowly recovered. The eye socket, it's true, looked awful. But he no longer appeared to suffer any pain. He went about the house as usual. As might be expected, however, he ran in terror whenever I came near.

At first I was hurt that a creature who had once loved me now disliked me so much. But this feeling soon gave way to annoyance.

One morning, I slipped a noose around its neck and hung it from a tree. I hung it with tears streaming from my eyes and with bitter sorrow at my heart. I hung it *because* I knew that it had loved me, and *because* I knew I had no reason to do so.

That night I was awakened from sleep by the cry of fire. The curtains of my bed were in flames. The whole house was blazing. My wife, my servant, and myself escaped with great difficulty. The destruction was complete. My entire worldly wealth burned to the ground.

On the day after the fire, I visited the ruins. The walls, with one exception, had fallen in. This exception was a wall in the middle of the house, where the head of my bed had rested. This wall had not burned as the others because it had been recently plastered.

A big crowd surrounded the wall. Many people seemed to be looking at a certain part of it very closely. Hearing the words "strange!" and "odd!" made me curious. I went nearer and saw the figure of a gigantic cat with a rope around its neck.

When I first saw this sight, I was terrified. When I thought more about it, I felt better. I remembered that the cat had been hung in a garden next to the house. When the cry of fire had been heard, the garden had quickly filled with people. Someone must have cut the animal loose and thrown it through an open window into my room. Perhaps this had been done to wake me up. The falling of the other walls had pressed the cat into the newly laid plaster. And so, the picture had been made.

While this explained the event, it still bothered me. For months I could not get rid of the sight of the cat. During this time I also began to experience a feeling that seemed, but wasn't, sorrow for what I had done. I even began to feel regret for the loss of the animal. I started to look about the places I now visited for another cat to take its place.

One night I sat half-drunk in an evil pub, when my attention was drawn to a black object. It sat on one of the large barrels of gin or rum. I went up to it and touched it with my hand. It was a black cat. It was as large as Pluto, and it looked like him in every way but one. Pluto did not have a white hair on his whole body. This cat had a large spot of white covering almost his entire breast.

When I touched him, he quickly rose. He purred loudly, rubbed against my hand, and

appeared delighted with me. This, then, was the very animal I was searching for. I offered to buy it from the landlord. But he knew nothing of the cat and had never seen it before.

When I left to go home, the animal followed me. I allowed it to do so. When it reached the house, it made itself right at home and became a favorite with my wife right away.

As for me, I soon began to dislike it. This was just the opposite of what I had expected. It seemed that its fondness for me caused me to feel disgusted and annoyed.

I avoided the creature. A sense of shame from my earlier crime stopped me from hurting it. For some weeks, I did not injure it in any way. But slowly I came to look upon it with a deep hatred.

One thing added to my hatred of the beast. That was a discovery I had made on the morning after I had brought it home. This cat, like Pluto, had lost one of its eyes. This fact had made my wife even more fond of the animal. Her nature was marked by a great gentleness and kindness.

The more I disliked the cat, however, the more it seemed to like me. Wherever I sat, it would crouch under my chair. If I got up to walk, it would get between my feet and nearly trip me. At such times I wished to destroy it with a single blow. I was stopped from doing so partly by the memory of my earlier crime—but mostly by an absolute *dread* of the beast.

It is hard to say what this dread was. I am almost ashamed to say—yes, even in this prison cell—I am ashamed to say what caused this dread. My wife had mentioned more than once the white spot on the animal's breast. The shape of this spot had begun to slowly change. It changed so slowly that at first I thought I was only imagining it.

Finally it began to take a definite shape. It now looked like an object which I shudder to name. It was the image of a horrible NOOSE! For this, above all, I dreaded the animal and would have killed the monster *had I dared.*

I knew no rest, either by day or night. During the day, the creature would not leave me alone. At night, I often had terrible dreams. When I woke, the hot breath of the *thing* was upon my face. And its huge weight was always upon my *heart!*

Under these pressures, the little good that was left in me disappeared. I began to hate all things and all people. Throughout all this my kind and gentle wife suffered the worst of it.

One day she went with me on some household errand. We went into the cellar of the old building we now lived in. The cat followed me down the stairs. When it nearly caused me to fall, I became enraged. I picked up an axe and aimed a blow at the animal.

If I had struck it, the cat would certainly have died. But the blow was stopped by my wife's hand. I was furious because she interfered. I withdrew my arm from her hold and buried the axe in her brain. She fell dead upon the spot, without a groan.

The awful murder was done with. Now I had to go about the job of hiding the body. I knew I could not remove it from the house, either by day or night. I could not risk being seen by the neighbors. I thought about many different ways of doing it. Finally, I came up with what I thought was a very good plan. I would wall the body up in the cellar.

The cellar was perfect for what I had in mind. Its walls were loosely built. They had recently been plastered, and the damp air kept the rough plaster from getting hard. In addition, there was a fireplace that had been filled up and made to look like the rest of the cellar. I knew I could remove some bricks, place the corpse inside, and then replace the bricks. No eye would be able to see anything suspicious.

I used a crowbar to remove the bricks. I carefully placed the body, standing up, against the inner wall. Then I re-laid the whole structure as it originally stood. When I finished, I was satisfied that all was right.

My next step was to look for the beast who had been the cause of so much misery. I had firmly decided to put it to death. However, the smart animal had been scared off by my violence. It had disappeared. It is impossible to describe the deep joy I felt by the hated creature's absence. It did not return during the night. So, for one night at least, I slept soundly— even with the burden of murder upon my soul!

The second and third day passed. And still the hated beast did not come. The monster, in terror, had fled the house forever! My happiness was complete! The guilt of my dark deed bothered me very little. A few questions had been asked, but they had been easily answered. A search had even been conducted—but of course nothing was discovered. I thought my future was safe.

On the fourth day, the police came once again to investigate. I was not worried, however. The officers asked me to accompany them in their search. For the third or fourth time, they went into the cellar. I was calm. I walked back and forth freely. The police were fully satisfied and ready to leave. The joy at my heart was too much to hold in.

I had to say one word—in triumph—to leave them no doubt of my innocence. "By the way, gentlemen," I said as they turned to go up the steps, "this is a very well-built house. These walls are solidly put together." Here I rapped heavily with a cane upon the very spot in the wall behind which stood the corpse of my wife.

May God protect me from the fangs of the devil! As soon as the sound from my blows had stopped, I was answered by a voice from within the tomb! It was a cry, at first muffled and broken. Then quickly it grew into one long, loud scream. It wasn't human. It was a howl of horror and of triumph.

I swooned and staggered to the opposite wall. At first the police didn't move, out of terror. Then a dozen arms were clawing at the wall. It fell heavily. The corpse, already decaying, stood straight up before the eyes of the police. Upon its head, with a red wide-open mouth and one eye of fire, sat the awful beast. The beast who had caused me to murder and whose voice had now sentenced me to hang. I had walled the monster up within the tomb!

The Oblong Box

Some years ago I booked passage on a ship from Charleston, South Carolina, to New York. The ship was called the *Independence,* and its captain was Captain Hardy. We were to sail on June 15th, weather permitting. The day before, I went aboard to arrange some matters in my stateroom.

I learned that we were going to have a great many passengers. On the list were several people I knew. Among these, I was pleased to see the name of Mr. Cornelius Wyatt. He was a young artist who had been my friend at the university. Wyatt was practically a genius, although he could be moody. He also had the warmest and truest heart a human being ever had.

I noticed that Wyatt's name was listed on *three* staterooms. I saw that he had booked passage for himself, his wife, and his two sisters. The staterooms were quite roomy, and each had two beds, one above the other.

I could not understand why there were *three* staterooms for these four persons. It was no business of mine, to be sure. Still, I set about trying to solve the puzzle. Finally, I thought I had the answer. "It is a servant, of course," I said.

"What a fool I am not to have seen it sooner."

Once again I looked at the list. But here I saw clearly that *no* servant was to come with the party. Yet, the original plan had been to bring one. The word *servant* had at first been written and then crossed out.

"Oh, it must be extra baggage," I now said to myself. "It is something he doesn't wish to put in the hold. It's something he wants to keep under his own eye. Ah, I have it—a painting—perhaps even the copy of the 'Last Supper' he has been trying to get." This idea satisfied me, and I thought no more about it.

I knew Wyatt's two sisters very well. They were friendly and clever young women. Wyatt had recently married, and I had not yet met his wife. He had often talked about her to me, however. He described her as a woman of great beauty and wit. So I was quite anxious to meet her.

On the day I visited the ship—June 14th— Wyatt and his party were also to visit it. I waited around for an extra hour in the hope of meeting his wife. But then an apology came. "Mrs. Wyatt was a little ill. She would not come aboard until tomorrow, at the hour of sailing."

The next day arrived. I was going from my hotel to the wharf when I met Captain Hardy. He said that "owing to circumstances"—a stupid but necessary phrase—the *Independence* would not sail for a day or two. He said that when all was ready he would send a message to let me know.

I did not receive the captain's message for nearly a week. It came finally, and I immediately went on board. Wyatt's party arrived about ten minutes after I did. There were the two sisters, the bride, and the artist—who was in one of his bad moods. I was somewhat used to these, so I didn't pay much attention to it. He did not even introduce me to his wife. This job fell to his sister Marian. In a few hurried words, she made us acquainted.

Mrs. Wyatt's face had been covered by a veil. She raised it to respond to my bow. When she did, I must confess I was very surprised.

The truth is she was a very plain-looking woman. If she wasn't positively ugly, she was not very far from it. She was dressed, however, beautifully. I had no doubt that she'd captured my friend's heart because of her intelligence and her good soul. She said very few words and went at once to her stateroom with Wyatt.

My old curiosity returned. There was no servant—*that* was settled. So I looked for the extra baggage. After some delay, a cart arrived at the wharf with an oblong pine box. As soon as it arrived, we set sail.

As I said, the box was oblong. It was about six feet in length and about two and a half in width. Now this shape was odd. As soon as I saw it, I knew my earlier guess had been right. The box had to contain a painting. I thought the matter was finally settled.

One thing bothered me, though. The box did *not* go into the extra stateroom. It was put into Wyatt's own room. It remained there and took up almost the whole floor. On the box's lid were painted the following words: *Mrs. Adelaide Curtis, Albany, New York. Charge of Cornelius Wyatt. This side up. Handle with care.*

Now I knew that Mrs. Adelaide Curtis was the artist's mother-in-law. Why would the painting be sent to her? I looked upon the entire address as a mystery, intended just for me. I made up my mind, of course, that the box would never get farther north than my friend's studio on Chambers Street, New York.

For the first three days we had fine weather. So the passengers were in a good mood and were quite friendly. I *must* say that included everyone but Wyatt and his sisters. They behaved stiffly and were mostly unfriendly to the rest of the party.

Wyatt was gloomy, even beyond his usual ways. Still, I was prepared for his moods. His sisters were another matter. They kept to their stateroom during most of the voyage. And they refused to talk with anyone on board, even though I urged them to do so.

Mrs. Wyatt was far more friendly. She became friendly with most of the ladies and even some of the men. She amused us all very much. The truth is I soon learned that Mrs. Wyatt was more often laughed *at* than *with*. She was said to be "a good-hearted thing, plain-looking, uneducated, and somewhat vulgar."

The great wonder was how Wyatt had been trapped into such a match. Wealth was everyone's general answer. But I knew that was no answer at all. Wyatt had told me his wife had not brought him a dollar.

He had married, he said, "for love, and for love only." And his bride "was more than worthy of his love." When I thought of my friend's words, I was very puzzled. Was it possible that he was losing his mind? What else could I think?

One day he came up on deck. I took his arm, and we walked together back and forth. He was still quite gloomy. He said very little, and that was with great effort. I tried a joke or two, and he made an attempt to smile. Poor fellow! I thought of his *wife* and wondered that he could smile at all.

Finally, I brought up the oblong box. I began a series of comments about it. My aim was to let him know, bit by bit, that I was not to be fooled about its contents. I said something about the "odd shape of *that* box." As I spoke these words I smiled, winked, and poked him gently in the ribs.

The way Wyatt took my comments convinced me he was mad. At first, he stared at me as if he didn't get the meaning of my words. Then a moment later, as he understood them, his eyes seemed to bulge from their sockets. He grew very red, then quite pale. He began to laugh loudly. He continued this way for about ten minutes. Finally, he fell face down on the deck. When I ran up to him, he seemed *dead*.

I called for help. After a while, he came to. But

for a time, he didn't make much sense when he spoke. Then we put him to bed. The next morning he had recovered. At least his body had. Of course, I can say nothing of his mind.

I avoided him for the rest of the trip, on the advice of the captain. He seemed to agree with my opinion of Wyatt's mind. But he asked me to say nothing about it to anyone else on board.

Several other things happened after this to add to my curiosity. For two nights I could not sleep very well. My stateroom opened into the main cabin, as did those of all the other single men on board. Wyatt's three rooms connected to the after-cabin. It was separated from the main one by a sliding door. This door was never locked, even at night.

The tossing of the ship often caused the sliding door between the cabins to slide open. It stayed that way because no one got up to shut it. When my stateroom door was open, as well as the sliding door, I could see quite clearly into the after-cabin. In fact, I could see exactly where Wyatt's staterooms were.

Those two nights while I lay awake, I clearly saw Mrs. Wyatt leave her husband's stateroom at about eleven o'clock. She entered the extra room, where she stayed until daybreak. Then she was called by her husband and went back. That they were separated was clear. They had

separate rooms and were probably heading for divorce. Here, finally, was the mystery of the extra stateroom.

One other thing that happened during those nights interested me. After Mrs. Wyatt had gone into the extra stateroom, I could hear noises coming from Wyatt's room. After listening for a while, I determined what they were.

The artist was prying open the oblong box and removing the lid. He used a chisel and a mallet. He had obviously tried to muffle the noise by covering the mallet's head with some cotton or wool.

After this there was a dead silence. I heard nothing more until daybreak, unless I mention what sounded like a low sobbing or sighing sound. I say it sounded like sobbing or sighing, but of course it couldn't have been either. I think it was just a ringing in my ears.

Wyatt had simply opened the box to gaze at his art treasure inside. There was nothing in this, however, to make him *sob*. That's why I say it must have been my imagination. In the morning I heard him put the lid back on the box. Then he came out of his stateroom, fully dressed, and called Mrs. Wyatt from hers.

We had been at sea for seven days and were now off Cape Hatteras. At that point we caught a heavy wind from the southwest. We were prepared for it, though. The weather had been threatening for some time. Everything was tightened and secured as the wind steadily increased.

We rode safely enough for 48 hours. At the end of this time, however, the storm had become a hurricane. One sail split into ribbons, and we took on a lot of water. We lost three men overboard and part of the ship above the upper deck. We hardly had recovered from this when we lost another sail.

The ship continued to take on water. To make matters worse, the pumps became clogged and were nearly useless. Meanwhile the leak gained on us very fast.

It was decided finally to abandon the ship. After much hard work, we were able to get the longboat over the side without an accident. The entire crew and most of the passengers crowded into the boat. This party took off right away. They arrived at Ocracoke Inlet in three days.

The captain and 14 passengers remained on board. This group decided to try their luck with the smaller boat at the ship's stern. The boat was lowered without much difficulty, though it nearly turned over when it hit the water. I was among the group in this boat. In addition to the captain and his wife, the group included Wyatt and his entire party.

We took a few necessary tools, some food, and the clothes upon our backs. No one had even thought of trying to save anything more. We were shocked then when Wyatt stood up in the boat just as we pulled away from the ship. He demanded that Captain Hardy move the boat back so he could take along the oblong box.

"Sit down, Mr. Wyatt," the captain said sternly. "You will capsize us if you do not sit still."

"The box!" Wyatt yelled. "The box I say! Captain Hardy, you cannot, you *will* not refuse me."

For a moment the captain seemed touched by Wyatt's pleading. Then he recovered and spoke calmly.

"Mr. Wyatt, you are mad. I cannot listen to you. Sit down, I say, or you will swamp the boat. Stay—hold him, seize him! He is about to spring overboard. There—I knew it—he is over!"

As the captain said this, Wyatt in fact jumped from the boat. He managed, by almost superhuman strength, to get hold of a rope hanging from the ship. A moment later he was on board, rushing down into the cabin.

We tried to get back close to the ship. But our little boat was pushed farther and farther away by the rough seas.

Our distance from the wreck increased quickly. Wyatt came back on deck dragging the oblong box with him. We watched, amazed, as he tied a three-inch rope first around the box and then around his body. In another moment, both the body and box were in the sea. They disappeared suddenly, once and forever.

We remained a while, our eyes sadly fixed on the spot. Finally, we pulled away. No one spoke for an hour. Then I said, "Did you notice, Captain, how suddenly they sank? Wasn't that an unusual thing?"

"They sank as a matter of course," the captain said. "They will soon rise again, however—*but not till the salt melts.*"

"The salt?" I shouted.

"Hush," he said, pointing to Wyatt's wife and sisters. "We must talk of these things at a better time."

We suffered much and made a narrow escape. After four days, we landed on the beach opposite Roanoke Island. We stayed here a week and then booked passage to New York.

About a month later, I happened to meet Captain Hardy on Broadway. He then explained the entire matter of Wyatt and the oblong box.

The artist had booked passage for himself, wife, two sisters, and servant. His wife was, as she had been described, a most lovely woman. On the morning of June 14th, the lady suddenly became ill and died. The young husband was filled with grief. He could not, however, delay his trip to New York.

Now, he also had to take the corpse of his beloved wife to her mother. But to do so openly was out of the question. Most of the passengers would have abandoned the ship rather than sail with a dead body.

Captain Hardy came up with a solution. The corpse was first partially embalmed, then packed with a large amount of salt. It was placed in the oblong box and marked as cargo. It was known that Wyatt had booked passage for his wife, so it was necessary for someone to play her role. The dead woman's maid was easily called upon to do so. During the day, she performed, as best she could, the part of her dead mistress. At night she slept in the extra stateroom.

My own mistake came from too careless and curious a nature. But lately, I rarely sleep soundly at night. There is the red face of Wyatt that haunts me. And there is his crazed laugh that will ring in my ears forever.

The Cask of Amontillado

The man Fortunato had done me a thousand wrongs. And I had put up with them as best I could. But when he started to insult me, I vowed revenge. I did not utter a threat, though. You who know the nature of my soul so well must know that. In time, I would set things right. And, I would do it and not suffer any punishment for it.

I did not give Fortunato any reason to suspect me. I continued to smile in his face. He could not know that my smile was *now* at the thought of his death.

In many ways Fortunato was a man to be respected and feared. But he had a weak point. He took pride in his expert knowledge of wine. In this matter, he and I had something in common. I was an expert in the Italian wines myself. I bought them in casks, or barrels, whenever I could.

Early one evening, during the mad carnival season, I met my friend. He greeted me very warmly, for he had been drinking heavily. He had on a jester's costume. On his head was a cone-shaped cap with bells on it.

"My dear Fortunato," I said, shaking his hand.

"How very well you are looking today. I have received a cask of what passes for amontillado. But I have my doubts."

"How?" he said. "Amontillado? A cask? Impossible! And in the middle of the carnival!"

"I have my doubts," I said. "And I was silly enough to pay the full amontillado price without talking to you first. You were not to be found. And I was afraid of losing a bargain."

"Amontillado!"

"I have my doubts," I said. "I must satisfy them. You are busy. I am on my way to see Luchresi. If anyone can tell, it is he. He will—"

"Luchresi cannot tell amontillado from sherry."

"And yet some fools will say that his taste is a match for your own."

"Come, let's go," he said.

"Where?"

"To your vaults," he answered.

"My friend, no," I said. "I will not take advantage of your good nature. I think you have some place to go. Luchresi—"

"I have no place to go—come," he said.

"No, my friend. I see you have a bad cold. The vaults are very damp."

"Let us go anyway. The cold is nothing. Amontillado! You have been taken advantage of. And as for Luchresi, he cannot tell sherry from amontillado." With that, he took my arm and led me toward my home.

My servants were not at home. They had left to attend the carnival. I'd told them I would not return until morning. I had given them orders not to leave the house. I knew these orders were good enough to make sure they *would* leave as soon as my back was turned.

I took two torches and gave one to Fortunato. Then we walked through several rooms to the archway that led into the vaults. We went down a winding staircase and stood upon the damp ground of the catacombs.

My friend's walk was unsteady. The bells upon his cap jingled as he walked.

"The cask," he said. Ugh! ugh! ugh!

"It is farther on," I said. "By the way, how long have you had that cough?"

He turned toward me. His eyes had the look of someone who was drunk. My poor friend could not answer for many minutes because of his cough.

"Ugh! ugh! ugh! It is nothing," he said at last.

"Come, we will go back," I said. "Your health is important. You are rich, admired, and loved. You are happy as I once was. You are a man to be missed. We will go back; you will be ill. Besides, there is Luchresi—"

"Enough," he said. "The cough is nothing. It will not kill me."

"True," I replied. "But you should be careful. A drink of this Medoc will protect us from the dampness." I took a bottle of wine from a long row. "Drink," I said, handing him the wine.

He raised it to his lips. "I drink to the buried that lie around us," he said.

"And I to your long life," I answered.

He took my arm again, and we walked on.

"These vaults are quite large," he said.

"The Montresors were a large and important family," I said.

The wine sparkled in his eyes. My own body grew warm from the Medoc. We had passed through long walls of piled skeletons mixed in with large casks. I stopped again and grabbed Fortunato by his arm.

"Moisture drips among the bones!" I said. "It is very damp. Come, we will go back before it is too late. Your cough—"

"It is nothing," he said. "Let us go on. But first, another drink of the Medoc."

I gave him another bottle. He emptied it at once. His eyes flashed with a fierce light. He laughed and threw the bottle upward with a gesture I did not understand. I looked at him in surprise.

"You do not understand?" he said.

"No," I replied.

"Then you are not of the brotherhood?"

"Who?"

"You are not of the masons?"

"Yes, yes," I said.

"You? A mason? Impossible!"

"A mason," I replied.

"Show me a sign," he said.

"It is this," I said. And I produced a trowel from under my cloak.

"You joke," he cried. "But let us proceed to the amontillado."

"So we shall," I said. I put the tool beneath the cloak again. I offered him my arm, and he leaned on it heavily. We walked down, down until we arrived at a deep crypt. The air was foul.

At the far end of the crypt was another smaller one. Its walls had been lined with human remains. On three sides of the crypt, bodies were piled all the way up to the vault above.

The bones from the fourth side had been removed, leaving an open space. In this wall cleared of bones was an alcove about four feet deep, three feet wide, and six or seven feet high. Behind it was a wall of solid stone.

"Ah, here we are," I said at last.

Fortunato tried hard to see inside the alcove.

But the torch's flame had dulled, and there was not enough light.

"Go on," I said. "Inside is the amontillado. As for Luchresi—"

"He is a fool," my friend said. He moved forward with an unsteady step. I followed right at his heels. When he hit the stone wall, he stood still, puzzled.

On the wall's surface were two iron rings. From one ring hung a short chain. From the other, hung a padlock. I threw the chain around his waist and secured it. Within seconds, I had him chained to the wall. He was too shocked to fight me. I withdrew the key and stepped back.

"Pass your hand over the wall," I said. "You cannot help feeling the mold. It is *very* damp. Once more let me *beg* you to go back. No? Then I must leave you. But first I will do what little I can for you."

"The amontillado," my friend cried. He had not yet recovered from his shock.

"Yes, the amontillado," I replied.

I walked over to the pile of bones on the ground. I threw them aside and uncovered some building stone and mortar. With these materials and my trowel, I began to wall up the entrance to the alcove.

I had hardly laid the first row of stones when I discovered that Fortunato's drunkenness had worn off. I could hear a low, moaning cry from deep inside. It was *not* the cry of a drunken man. There was a long silence. I laid several more rows of stone. Then I heard the furious shaking of the chains. I stopped working and sat upon the bones.

When the clanging stopped I resumed my work. When I had laid several more rows, I threw a weak light upon the figure inside. There was a series of loud, harsh screams from the throat of the chained man. This went on for some time.

By midnight my work was almost finished. When I had nearly put the last stone in place, I heard a low laugh from inside. It was followed by a sad voice. I had trouble recognizing it as that of the noble Fortunato. The voice said, "Ha, ha, a very good joke indeed. We will have many a rich laugh about it over our wine."

"The amontillado," I said.

"He! he! Yes, the amontillado. But isn't it getting late? They will be waiting for us—the Lady Fortunato and the rest. Let us be gone."

"Yes," I said, "let us be gone."

"*For the love of God, Montresor!*" he pleaded.

"Yes, for the love of God," I said.

I listened for a reply. It did not come. I called aloud "Fortunato!" No answer. I called again. "Fortunato!"

Still no answer. I thrust a torch through the

remaining opening and let it fall in. In return, there came only a jingling of bells. My heart grew sick. It was the dampness of the place that made it so.

I hurried to finish my work. I forced the last stone into place and plastered it up. I moved the old stack of bones against the wall. For 50 years, no man has disturbed them. *May he rest in peace!*